MW00745653

For My Wife

Compiled by
Liesl Santiago

PETER PAUPER PRESS, INC.
WHITE PLAINS · NEW YORK

For my parents

Copyright © 1994
Peter Pauper Press, Inc.
202 Mamaroneck Avenue
White Plains, NY 10601
All rights reserved
ISBN 0-88088-785-0
Printed in Hong Kong
7   6   5   4   3   2

FOR MY WIFE

I'm a pretty smart fellow. Once I found her, I was smart enough not to let her go.

George Burns,
on Gracie Allen

*O*ne of the best hearing aids a man can have is an attentive wife.

Groucho Marx

*W*omen [have] a special
talent for understanding a
man better than he under-
stands himself.

Victor Hugo

A good marriage is at least 80 percent good luck in finding the right person at the right time. The rest is trust.

Nanette Newman

*A*n occasional lucky guess as to what makes a wife tick is the best a man can hope for. Even then, no sooner has he learned how to cope with the tick than she tocks.

Ogden Nash

*M*y wife doesn't care what I do when I'm away, as long as I don't have a good time.

Lee Trevino

*T*ry praising your wife,
even if it does frighten her
[at] first.

Billy Sunday

*I*t would have been
impossible for any ordinary
man to have got through
what I have had to get
through, in peace and war,
without her devoted aid.

Winston Churchill,
about his wife, Clementine

A man's wife has
more power over him than
the state has.

Ralph Waldo Emerson

*W*hat is instinct? It is
the natural tendency in one
when filled with dismay to
turn to his wife.

Finley Peter Dunne

I have been supportive of my wife since the beginning of time, and she has been supportive of me. It's not sacrifice; it's family.

Martin D. Ginsburg,
husband of
Justice Ruth Bader Ginsburg

*Y*our wife will defend you like the bear in the fable of La Fontaine; she will throw paving stones at your head to drive away the flies that alight on it.

Honoré de Balzac

*L*ove is when you're married twenty-five years, smooching in your living room, and he runs out of gas and she still says she loves him. That's love!

Norm Crosby

$\mathcal{M}$y wife is as handsome as when she was a girl, and I, a poor nobody then, fell in love with her; and what is more, I have never fallen out.

Abraham Lincoln,
on Mary Todd Lincoln

$\mathcal{W}$e are one, after all,
you and I, together we suffer,
together exist, and forever
will recreate each other.

Teilhard de Chardin

*F*rom the moment I met her, it was magic. I actually bought a diamond a week later but didn't show it to her until six-and-a-half years later.

Kenny G

There are feelings
which women guess in spite
of the care men take to bury
them.

Honoré de Balzac

*T*he first thing I did
when I saw Nicole, I turned
to my accountant and said,
"*Her* I would marry
tomorrow—*without* a
prenuptial."

Eddie Murphy

*N*othing new here
except my marrying, which
to me is a matter of profound
wonder.

Abraham Lincoln

I'd like to dispel the myth that when you put a wedding ring on a woman, her brain stops.

Marilyn Quayle

Sometimes idiosyncrasies which used to be irritating become endearing, part of the complexity of a partner who has become woven deep into our own selves.

Madeleine L'Engle

The only way our relationship will run smoothly is for me to understand that guys will be after her. So we have to trust each other—and we have that trust.

David Justice,
about his wife, Halle Berry

*W*e had a good marriage. We knew it was a good marriage because we never read anything bad about it in the papers.

George Burns

I'm amazed at how
marriage focuses your energy.
. . . The trust and respect that
comes out of a serious
partnership with the other
person is great.

Richard Gere

$\mathcal{B}$ut monogamy is not merely a good event; it is a good habit.

G. K. Chesterton

*M*arriage is not a finished affair. No matter to what age you live, love must be continuously consolidated. Being considerate, thoughtful and respectful without ulterior motives is the key to a satisfactory marriage.

Pamphlet from Chinese
Family Planning Center

$\mathcal{F}$or me, marriage is
life's most wonderful
experience.

Kevin Costner

A man without a wife
is like a man without hands.

Ukrainian Proverb

*A*ny young man who is unmarried at the age of twenty-one is a menace to the community.

Brigham Young

*B*ecause his wife is of such a delicate nature, a man avoids using certain words all through his married life, and then one day he picks up a bestseller she is reading and finds five of the words in the first chapter.

William Feather

*N*othing flatters a man
as much as the happiness of
his wife; he is always proud
of himself as the source of it.

Samuel Johnson

*N*o happiness is like
unto it, no love so great as
that of man and wife, no
such comfort as a sweet wife.

Robert Burton

*T*he luckiest thing that ever happened to me was the girl I married.

Dwight D. Eisenhower

*H*er success is my success.

Scott Holt,
on wife, Tracy Austin

*N*o man knows what
the wife of his bosom is until
he has gone with her through
the fiery trials of this world.

Washington Irving

*H*eaven will be no heaven to me if I do not meet my wife there.

Andrew Jackson

*M*arriage is give and take. You'd better give it to her or she'll take it anyway.

Joey Adams

*H*e that speaks ill of
his wife dishonors himself.

Thomas Fuller

*M*arriage enlarges the scene of our happiness and miseries. A marriage of love is pleasant; a marriage of interest, easy; and a marriage where both meet, happy. A happy marriage has in it all the pleasures of friendship, all the enjoyments of sense and reason, and, indeed, all the sweets of life.

Joseph Addison

*W*hen a woman's husband quits doing something he knows she doesn't like it is time for her to discover what he has been doing in its place.

Reflections of a Bachelor

$\mathcal{I}$f your wife is small,
stoop down and whisper in
her ear.

Jewish Proverb

*M*y wife thinks I'm too nosy. At least that's what she keeps scribbling in her diary.

Drake Sather

 $\mathcal{A}$ successful
marriage is not a gift; it is an
achievement.

Ann Landers

I find nothing more extravagant than to see a husband who is still in love with his wife.

Madeleine de Scudéry

*O*ne of the good things that come of a true marriage is that there is one face on which changes come without your seeing them; or rather there is one face which you can still see the same, through all the shadows which years have gathered upon it.

George Macdonald

How to Stay Together One More Day

Laugh at yourself and at each other.

Practice unselfishness.

Show your love.

Talk to, not at, each other.

Respond lovingly to his or her request.

Greet and leave each other with kind words.

Criticize the action, not the person.

Hold hands.

Resolve the day's differences before bedtime.

Admit your failings and ask for forgiveness.

Don't fight dirty.

Enjoy the present and welcome the future.

Make love, not waves.

*L*earn to bend. It's
better than breaking.

Leo Buscaglia

*W*hen a man brings
his wife flowers for no
reason—there's a reason.

Marion Jordan
(Molly McGee)

There is a lot to get used to in the first year of marriage. One wakes up in the morning and finds a pair of pigtails on the pillow that were not there before.

Martin Luther

*I*t is a matter of life and death for married people to interrupt each other's stories for if they did not, they would burst.

Logan Pearsall Smith

A woman springs a
sudden reproach upon you
which provokes a hot retort—
and then she will presently
ask you to apologize.

Mark Twain

*T*he husband who doesn't tell his wife everything probably reasons that what she doesn't know won't hurt him.

Leo J. Burke

*W*e would have broken up except for the children. Who were the children? Well, she and I were.

Mort Sahl

*O*ne is very crazy when in love.

Sigmund Freud

I've only had one argument with her in all our years together, but for just two people, we've kept it going pretty good.

George Gobel

*W*e are each of us
angels with only one wing.
And we can only fly
embracing each other.

Luciano de Crescenzo

*F*at tends to make a man a better husband. His wife is generally happy in the knowledge she is not married to a woman chaser. Few fat men chase girls, because they get winded too easily.

Hal Boyle

*P*eople say they're "in love," but I think marriage also requires respect and commitment. There are *always* going to be distractions. But you have to ask yourself: Who's more important, the person you married or this distraction? I happen to love my wife. It's as simple as that.

Bill Cosby

It's a big advantage to have someone who is smart. She's not afraid to express her opinion, even though it's not always what I want to hear. I have enough people around me who are yes-people. That's the last thing I need in a wife.

Arnold Schwarzenegger

I love marriage. A
woman by herself is a
perfectly asinine way to live.

Bette Davis

*A*ny list of the world's most beautiful women that doesn't mention my wife Kim isn't worth the paper it's printed on.

Hank Graham

There is nothing nobler or more admirable than when two people who see eye to eye keep house as man and wife, confounding their enemies and delighting their friends.

Homer,
The Odyssey

*T*he most difficult year
of marriage is the one
you're in.

Franklin P. Jones

*R*emember that
your wife is not your mother
or your maid, but your
partner and friend.

Marian Wright Edelman

*L*ove is like a friendship caught on fire. In the beginning a flame, very pretty, often hot and fierce but still only light and flickering. As love grows older, our hearts mature and our love becomes as coals, deep-burning and unquenchable.

Bruce Lee

*M*y wife's jealousy is getting ridiculous. The other day she looked at my calendar and demanded to know who May was.

Rodney Dangerfield